Science to the Rescue

Lost in the Cave

Can science save your life?

Felicia Law
& Gerry Bailey

Crabtree Publishing Company
www.crabtreebooks.com

Crabtree Publishing Company
www.crabtreebooks.com
1-800-387-7650

PMB 59051, 350 Fifth Ave.
59th Floor,
New York, NY 10118

616 Welland Ave.
St. Catharines, ON
L2M 5V6

Published by Crabtree Publishing in 2016

Author: Felicia Law and Gerry Bailey

Illustrator: Leighton Noyes

Editors: Shirley Duke, Kathy Middleton

Proofreader: Wendy Scavuzzo

**Production coordinator and
  Prepress technician:** Tammy McGarr

Print coordinator: Margaret Amy Salter

Printed in Canada/102015/IH20150821

Photographs:
All images are Shutterstock unless otherwise stated.
Front cover main image- andreiuc88; top- Marian Dreher;
middle- gn fotografie; bottom- Nik Niklz
p1- andrey_l, p2- andreiuc88, p3 bottom- pichayasri; 21; Klara
Viskova; blambca; jehsomwang, p6/7 bottom- pichayasri; 21;
Klara Viskova; blambca; jehsomwang, p7 top- Kayo; bottom-
zebra0209, p8 top-Steve Allen; bottom- wikimedia.org/
Daniel Schwen, p8/9- Chow Shue Ma, p9 top- Tutti Frutti;
bottom- Marian Dreher, p10/11 bottom- pichayasri; 21; Klara
Viskova; blambca; jehsomwang, p11 top- happystock; bottom-
Vadim Petrakov, p12 top- mrotchua; bottom- mrotchua,
p12/13 Vitalii Nesterchuk, p14/15 bottom- pichayasri; 21;
Klara Viskova; blambca; jehsomwang, p16 top- Dario Lo
Presti; bottom- Jeff Schultes, p16/17- Joshua Haviv, p18/19
bottom- pichayasri; 21; Klara Viskova; blambca; jehsomwang,
p19 top- Jason Patrick Ross; middle left- gn fotografie; middle
right- OPIS Zagreb; bottom- Dario Lo Presti, p20/21- Eduard
Kyslynskyy, p21 top a- All-stock-photos; top b- Cosmin
Manci; top c- Kazakov Maksim; bottom a- Matt Jeppson;
bottom b- Dmitri Gomon, p22 top- wikimedia.org/Mnolf;
bottom- wikipedia.org/unknown author, p26 top- Nik Niklz;
bottom- dominique landau, p26/27 main image- nikitsin.
smugmug.com; bottom- pichayasri; 21; Klara Viskova;
blambca; jehsomwang, p28- Sementer, p28/29 bottom-
pichayasri; 21; Klara Viskova; blambca; jehsomwang,
p29- Adwo; 30/31 bottom- pichayasri; 21; Klara Viskova;
blambca; jehsomwang

Library and Archives Canada Cataloguing in Publication

Law, Felicia, author
    Lost in the cave / Felicia Law, Gerry Bailey.

(Science to the rescue)
Illustrator: Leighton Noyes.
Includes index.
Issued in print and electronic formats.
ISBN 978-0-7787-1677-8 (bound).--
ISBN 978-0-7787-1699-0 (paperback).--
ISBN 978-1-4271-7675-2 (pdf).--ISBN 978-1-4271-7671-4 (html)

    1. Stalactites and stalagmites--Juvenile literature. 2. Cave
animals--Adaptation--Juvenile literature. I. Bailey, Gerry, 1945-, author
II. Noyes, Leighton, illustrator III. Title. IV. Series: Science to the
rescue (St. Catharines, Ont.)

GB601.2.L38 2015   j551.44'7   C2015-903234-2
                                              C2015-903235-0

Library of Congress Cataloging-in-Publication Data

Law, Felicia, author.
 Lost in the cave / Felicia Law, Gerry Bailey ; illustrated by
Leighton Noyes.
     pages cm. -- (Science to the rescue)
 Includes index.
  ISBN 978-0-7787-1677-8 (reinforced library binding) --
 ISBN 978-0-7787-1699-0 (pbk.) --
 ISBN 978-1-4271-7675-2 (electronic pdf) --
 ISBN 978-1-4271-7671-4 (electronic html)
 1. Caves--Juvenile literature. 2. Caving accidents--Juvenile
literature. 3. Survival--Juvenile literature. 4. Speleology--Juvenile
literature. I. Bailey, Gerry, author. II. Noyes, Leighton, illustrator.
III. Title. IV. Series: Bailey, Gerry, 1945- Science to the rescue.

 GB601.2.L37 2016
 613.69--dc23
                                              2015025180

Contents

Joe and Dr. Bea's story   4

What is a cave? Parts of a cave   6

Amazing caves   8

Limestone, Karst   10

Shilin   11

Going down!   12

Mapping a cave   14

Dripped shapes   16

More dripped shapes   18

Cave life   20

Glistening glowworms   22

Cave paintings   24

Ice and water   26

Cave science   28

Glossary   30

Learn more...   31

Index   32

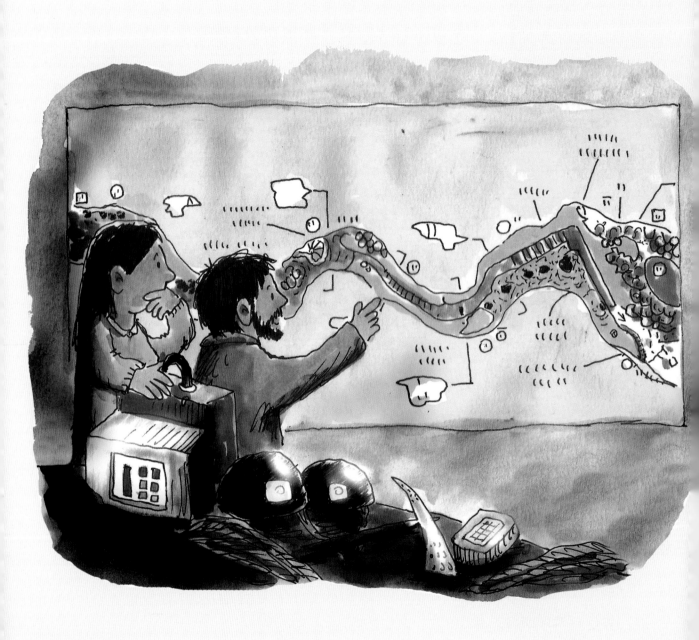

Joe and Dr. Bea's story

Hi! My name is Joe. Dr. Bea and I have just returned from the scariest of adventures! It all happened when we were exploring a cave —far below the mountain.

We had gone in to find some rare creatures that Dr. Bea had heard lived there. We had to go deep into the underground caves to find them, because they rarely ever left the safety of the dark.

But we found them—and much more, too. In fact, we got so excited by our finds that we almost forgot that caves are dangerous places.

But let me tell you what happened...

Dr. Bea told me she wanted to check out some worms living in a nearby cave. She thought they might be difficult to find. She said I could tag along if I wanted. She would welcome the help.

Because I had never climbed down into the depths of a cave before, I jumped at the chance to go with her.

What is a cave?

A cave is a natural underground opening or hollow space. Usually, caves are formed when water wears away rock, soil, or ice. In **limestone** rock, caves can become huge.

Parts of a cave

hole, called a sinkhole, created by the surface ground collapsing

underground stream

icicle-shaped mineral formation, called a stal

chamber

Caves are usually made up of large open areas called **chambers** or caverns. Caverns are joined by narrower systems lower down called passages.

The cave entrance may be a natural opening in the rock.

Formed over thousands of years as rock layers develop, most caves begin as natural underground hollows. The process of water **erosion** though cracks in the rock creates hollow areas that eventually form caves. Caves can also form along coastlines, where the action of crashing waves has the same eroding effect. A cave that forms in a **headland**, which is rock that juts out into the sea, can break through the other side of the rock to form an arch.

surface stream

pool in a chamber

limestone

passage

waterfall

The cave entrance may be carved out, or eroded, by the movement of waves and water.

Dr. Bea told me we could expect to see some rare and beautiful rock formations. It seems that some of the most amazing caves in the world have been discovered only recently. Many have had paths and railings added to them, so people can view inside safely without damaging the cave.

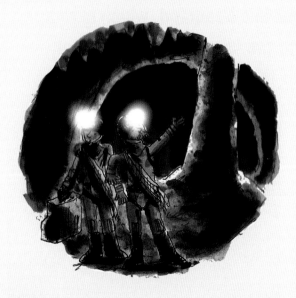

Amazing caves

Fingal's Cave in Ireland contains many six-sided columns of basalt rock.

Mammoth Cave in Kentucky is the longest cave in the world—more than 400 miles (644 km) long.

The famous Reed Flute Caves in Guilin, China, are lit with colored lights to show the different rock formations.

The Mulu Caves in Borneo contain one of the longest cave passages, as well as the Sarawak Chamber, which is nearly 1,970 feet (600 m) long and 262 feet (80 m) high.

The smooth walls of the Marble Caves in Chile appear blue because they reflect the lake's turquoise water.

Dr. Bea warned me the cave would be damp. Water seeped through cracks in the ceiling and fell on us in a constant drip.

This water was steadily wearing away the rocks and creating the amazing shapes that started to appear to us in the dark.

Limestone

Most large caves are found in areas with a soft rock called limestone. It is also known as chalk or **calcium carbonate**. Soft rock like this can be worn away, or eroded, by blowing winds and dripping water. These actions will eventually change the rock's shape. **Acid** in the water will also erode limestone and create a cave. Water is turned into a weak acid by the gas **carbon dioxide**, which is picked up from rotting plants.

Karst

Rocks dissolved by the weak acids in the water create a landscape called karst. Karst contains formations such as sinkholes, caves, underground streams, jutting rocks, or cliffs. The underground streams wear passages through the rock where the water drains away.

The Shilin stone forest in Jiuxiang, China, is an example of a karst landscape with shilin formations.

Shilin

Shilin formations are found in southern China. In fact, shilin means "stone forest" in the Chinese language. You can spot shilin easily because the tall rocks actually look like a forest of stone trees. These stone forests were formed around 270 million years ago.

It was time to start our descent down into a passage. The creatures that Dr. Bea wanted to find live in the darkest, coolest parts of the cave. To get there, we had to squeeze ourselves down one of the cracks.

We made sure our ropes were attached firmly to a rock. Our spiked shoes would stop us from slipping, but we still wanted to feel as safe as possible in this strange environment.

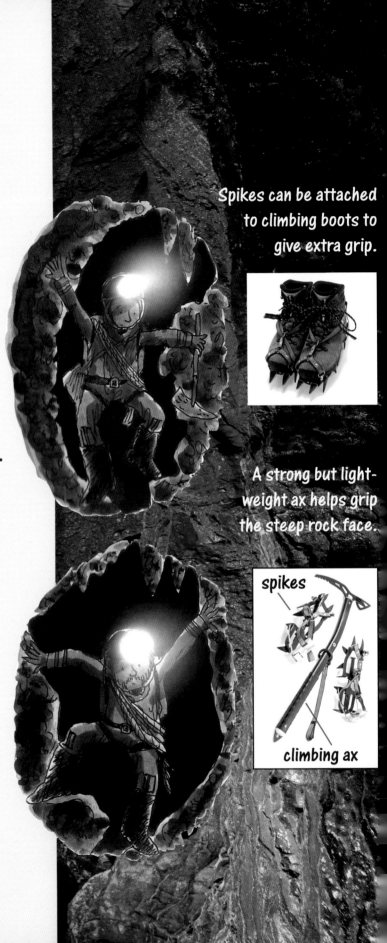

Spikes can be attached to climbing boots to give extra grip.

A strong but light-weight ax helps grip the steep rock face.

spikes

climbing ax

12

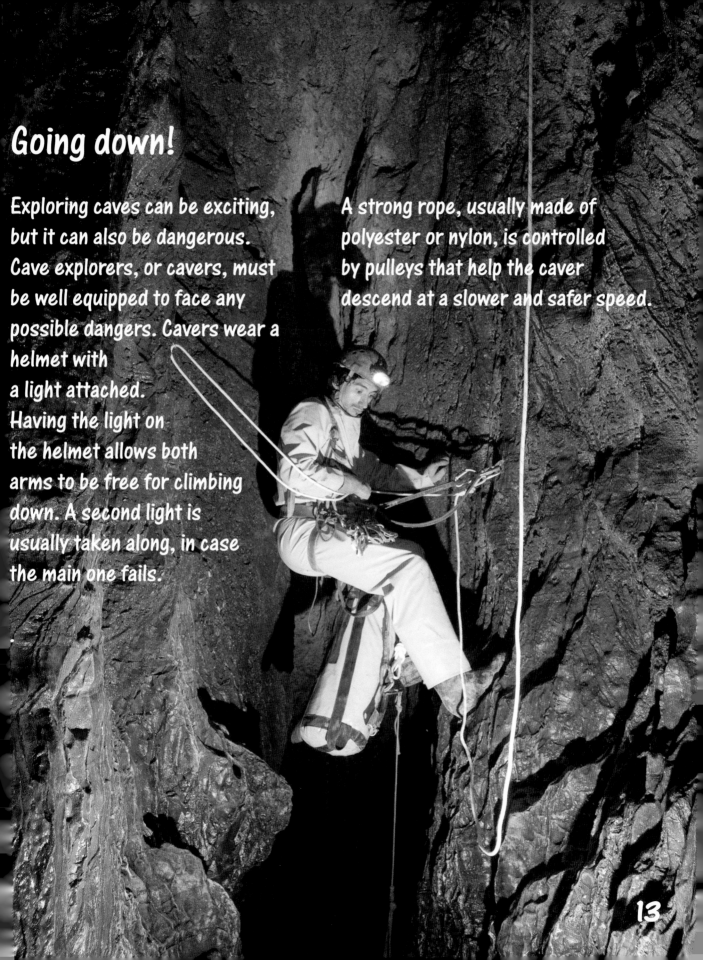

Going down!

Exploring caves can be exciting, but it can also be dangerous. Cave explorers, or cavers, must be well equipped to face any possible dangers. Cavers wear a helmet with a light attached. Having the light on the helmet allows both arms to be free for climbing down. A second light is usually taken along, in case the main one fails.

A strong rope, usually made of polyester or nylon, is controlled by pulleys that help the caver descend at a slower and safer speed.

13

Soon, we had made it through the crack and discovered that we were in a large chamber—larger than the chamber we had entered first.

Dr. Bea took out her measuring tools. She wanted to create an accurate survey of the cave, with all its chambers and passages. That way, she would be able to create a map of her findings when the trip was finished.

Mapping a cave

All data is recorded to be analyzed later. The cave is measured, and the main features and formations are recorded on a map. Mapmaking is called **cartography**.

Each new chamber is measured using modern measuring equipment, including lasers. Laser measuring equipment is accurate to one hundredth of an inch (0.025 cm).

These symbols are used on the map to identify what the scientists find:

boulders

stalactite

stalagmite

column

ledge

pool

narrow passage

pile of stones

crystals

sand and gravel

Special cameras are needed because there is little or no artificial light in a cave. The camera must have a large lens to let as much light into the camera as quickly as possible.

The drips falling on my helmet were getting heavier. Looking up, I soon discovered why. Dr. Bea aimed her light at the ceiling and showed me the most wonderful sight—stalactites and stalagmites—rock formations that looked like icicles.

Dripped shapes

As the water and dissolved limestone drip through the cave ceiling, the carbon dioxide in the liquid **evaporates**. A hardened mineral called calcium carbonate is left behind, slowly building into long shapes as it drips and collects on the cave floor.

Stalactites are the structures that hang from the ceiling. Stalagmites are the structures on the floor.

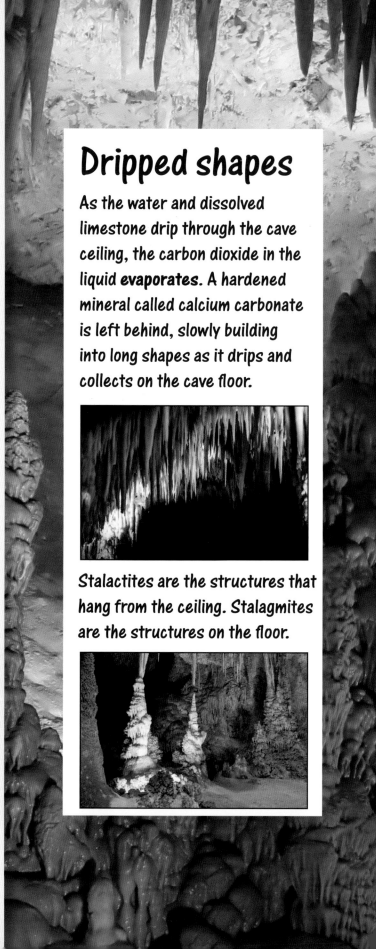

stalactites

cave ceiling

Lights have been added to this cave so the formations can be seen by visitors.

column

flowstone, a structure formed by water flowing down walls

stalagmite

cave floor

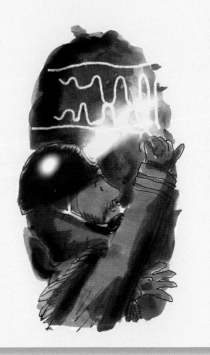

I wanted to study these fascinating formations up close. I moved from one to the other, marveling at how these hard mineral structures looked more like frozen water—sometimes even like waterfalls! When I realized I had wandered away from Dr. Bea, I decided to go back—but which way?

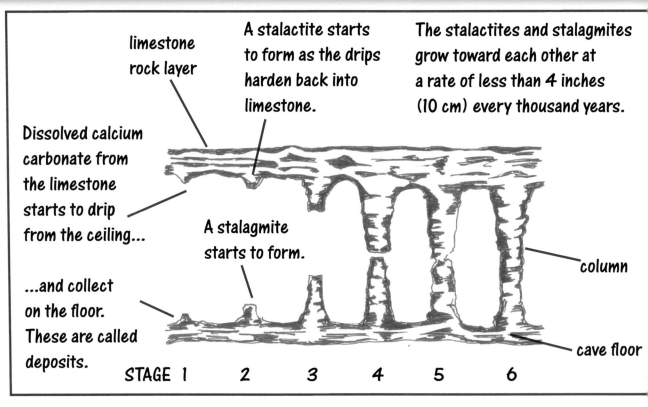

limestone rock layer

A stalactite starts to form as the drips harden back into limestone.

The stalactites and stalagmites grow toward each other at a rate of less than 4 inches (10 cm) every thousand years.

Dissolved calcium carbonate from the limestone starts to drip from the ceiling...

A stalagmite starts to form.

...and collect on the floor. These are called deposits.

column

cave floor

STAGE 1   2   3   4   5   6

More dripped shapes

Cave deposits are called speleothems or dripstone. Besides stalactites and stalagmites, there are many other different kinds of deposits.

Columns form when stalactites and stalagmites build up and meet. They look like pillars holding up the ceiling of the cave.

Flowstone is made up of **calcite** that is deposited in sheets. It forms when water flows down the walls or ceiling of a cave.

Straw stalactites occur at the start of a stalactite's life. They are long, thin tubes that point downward and come to a sharp point. Calcite

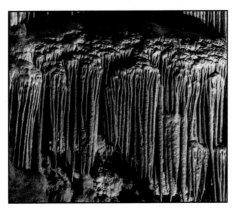

forms around a water drop on the cave ceiling, creating a tube. Water continues to run down inside the tube until it gets plugged, forming a typical stalactite.

Drapery deposits look like curtains made of rock. They are caused by calcite-rich water flowing along a cave ceiling. When the water loses its carbon dioxide, the calcite is deposited in thin trails that grow into wavy folds.

Suddenly, a pair of wings swished past my head. It was a bat! I aimed my light at the ceiling. The bats were difficult to see hanging up there. And I knew there were more than just bats living in this cave.

There are animals that live in caves that never leave—not even for food! They are known as troglobites. Dr. Bea had told me there were about 50,000 different species of troglobites in caves around the world—so many that no one will ever be able to discover them all.

True troglobites don't leave the cave. They are almost all blind—or nearly blind—and have no body color at all.

Cave life

Many animals live in caves. They include bats, birds, and tiny animals that can live without light.

Some animals, called trogloxenes, have to go out of the cave to eat. Bats are trogloxenes.

Other animals, such as small water dwellers and insects called troglobites, have adapted so that they can live their entire lives in caves.

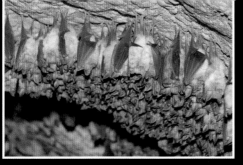
A colony of bats

Mexican tetras are fish that have no eyes and no color.

A pseudoscorpion

A bat

Bats live in caves all over the world. Some spend their lives in caves, while others hibernate there just to produce young. They leave the cave in large colonies at dusk to find insects to eat. Although they are not blind, bats use **echolocation** to find insect **prey**. They send out a high-pitched sounds that bounces off objects so they can "hear" where prey is.

A cave cricket

Some salamanders live in wet caves. Some have no eyes and some have no color.

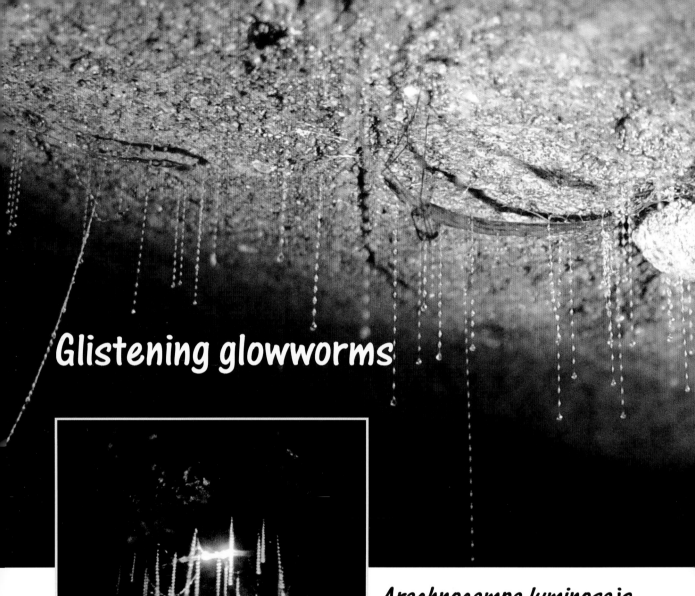

Glistening glowworms

The glowing lights and hanging, beaded threads of the glowworm *Arachnocampa luminosa* shine in the dark due to **bioluminescence.**

Arachnocampa luminosa is a species of glowworm that lives in caves in New Zealand. As grubs, these insect **larvae** make long strands of silk spit, or mucus. They hang like beaded webs to catch small flying insects.

Suddenly, I thought I saw a light moving in the tunnels. Was it Dr. Bea? I headed in that direction, hoping to find her. Cave systems are often a maze of passageways. This cave was no different.

I followed carefully from one chamber to another, and through one narrow passage to another. When I finally caught up to the light, I was extremely relieved to find that it was indeed coming from Dr. Bea's helmet.

She hadn't even noticed I had been missing. She was observing a small worm—and it was glowing! "You've found your worm!" I exclaimed. "I found more than that. Go take a look," she said.

Cave paintings

In the next chamber, an enormous painting filled the cave wall! Cave paintings have been discovered all over the world. Some were made about 35,000 years ago.

Most of the images had been sprayed on the wall. The ancient artist did this by grinding color **pigments** into powders and blowing them through a tube made of wood.

Megaloceros was a giant-sized elk that roamed across Europe, going as far as Siberia in the east. It was the largest elk that ever lived, and its huge antlers spanned almost 13 feet (4 m).

The *Coelodonta*, or woolly rhinoceros, had two huge horns on its snout—the front horn measuring up to 3 feet (1 m). Its shaggy coat helped it survive the harsh ice-age climate.

The huge cave bear was nearly 7 feet (2 m) long and lived in Europe during the last ice age. It probably escaped the terrible cold by hibernating in caves during the winter.

Homotherium, the saber-toothed cat, had two teeth that curved backward. Its front legs were longer than its back legs.

The woolly mammoth had long black, brown, orangey-red, or blond hair with an undercoat of finer hair. Its thick hair and a layer of fat helped keep it warm. Behind its head was a hump of fat that provided more energy during winter.

As we gazed at the **prehistoric** paintings, we heard the roar of water in the darkness.

We had moved right through the cave system to the entrance on the coast—the one often used by tourists coming to see the cave paintings. However, this entrance opened out into the sea—and the tide was coming in fast!

Ice and water

Caves can form in glacier ice, as well as forming in limestone. This happens at the snout, or front, of the glacier. When the glacier begins to melt, the meltwater runs toward its snout, carving out a passageway in the surrounding ice.

Ice can also form in ordinary limestone caves. If it becomes cold enough, water that trickles down into the cave will form needle-like icicles. The icicles can change in appearance from chamber to chamber. Ice formations, just like limestone formations, are known as speleothems.

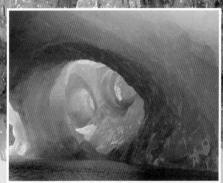

Caves formed in ice sheets are usually called glacier caves.

These needle-like icicles form when the temperature is below freezing and stays there. They are most often found in caves near a body of water that freezes in winter.

Dr. Bea knew the danger! Underwater caverns can fill with water very suddenly, leaving cavers cut off from escape. We had to beat the tide—and that meant finding a quick way out.

Luckily for us, the bats had the same idea. Their amazing ability to sense their way using echolocation drew them out of the cave through openings we had not spotted. They rose in a great cloud, leaving the cave to feed on insects in the evening sky. We quickly followed them out.

Cave science

The study of caves is known as speleology. Scientists who explore caves are called speleologists. Caves are interesting to scientists because they contain different **geological** materials.

Limestone rock often contains dazzling **crystals.** Crystals are unusually shaped minerals that were once molten, or liquid, but then cooled and hardened into flat-sided, geometric shapes in rock. The **molecules** that make up the cooling liquid fit together in a repeating pattern. This results in clear, shiny crystals.

Crystals form in different colors and shapes, depending on the materials that are in the liquid they are created from.

Speleologists study caves and karst features to determine the processes that formed them, how they changed over time, and what lives in them.

Limestone also traps the **fossils** of prehistoric plants and animals. Caves can be home to tiny **ecosystems** containing animal species that are ancient and rare—perhaps found in only a single cave.

Speleology covers lots of different sciences: chemistry, biology, geology, physics, meteorology, and cartography. Maps of caves made by speleologists show just how complicated and interesting these structures are.

That night Dr. Bea and I sat on the beach enjoying the warmth of a hot drink by our driftwood fire. We talked over the day's adventures.

Dr. Bea had found the beautiful glowworms that inhabit the cave, and I had discovered unexpected wonders there, too.

Glossary

acid A chemical substance that dissolves in water to make an acidic solution. Many acids can dissolve metals.

basalt A kind of rock or stone made from volcanic lava. It is a dark color and looks like it is made of very tiny pieces of rock. Basalt is one of the main kinds of rock that make up Earth's crust.

bioluminescence The light naturally given off by some living organisms, including fireflies, some deep-sea fish, and some cave animals

calcite A white or colorless mineral made up of crystals of calcium carbonate

calcium carbonate A salt that is made from carbon. It is the main part of limestone rock.

carbon dioxide A colorless gas with no smell and that can dissolve in water. It is released into the air from burning fossil fuels, and when animals exhale after using oxygen from the air.

cartography The process of making maps. A cartographer marks features of the land or sea on a map by symbols, contour lines, and shading.

chamber A large space in an underground cave or cavern

crystal A kind of mineral formed by cooling rock making geometrically shaped, flat-sided patterns

echolocation A way of using an echo to find hidden objects. Sound waves bounce off an object and return as echoes which help to show where the object is located.

ecosystem A group of animals, plants, and nonliving features in the same environment, growing and living together

erosion The moving or breaking down of rocks or soil, caused by the action of water, wind, or ice

evaporates Turns from a liquid into a vapor, or a gas

fossil The remains of a plant or animal that lived on Earth in a much earlier period of the planet's history and was preserved

geological Related to the study of Earth and its rocks

headland A narrow piece of land jutting out into the sea. Headlands often end in cliffs that fall steeply to the sea.

larva (plural is larvae) The young form of an insect

limestone A kind of rock formed from layers of sediment that have been pressed down into sedimentary rock over time

molecule The smallest particle of a substance

pigment The natural color that is in or comes from natural objects such as plants, animals, or soil

prey Animals that are hunted and killed by other animals for food

Learn more...

Books:

Caves
by Stephen Kramer. First Avenue Editions, 1995

Cave Animals
by Francine Galko. Heinemann, 2002

Caves and Caverns
by Gail Gibbons. HMH Books for Young Readers, 1996

Discovery in the Cave
by Mark Dubowski. Random House Books for Young Readers, 2010

Secrets of the Sky Caves: Danger and Discovery on Nepal's Mustang Cliffs
by Sandra K. Athans. Millbrook Press, 2014

Websites:

Information about caves, their formation, and life in them.
www.kidsdiscover.com/spotlight/caves-for-kids/

How caves are formed and the formations inside.
http://science.nationalgeographic.com/science/earth/surface-of-the-earth/
caves-article/

The science of caves.
http://teacher.scholastic.com/lessonrepro/lessonplans/theme/caves01.htm

Index

acid 10
animals 20–21, 22, 24–25, 29

basalt caves 8
bats 20–21, 28
bioluminescence 22

calcite 19
calcium carbonate 10, 16, 18
carbon dioxide 10, 16, 19
cartography 14–15, 29
cave bears 25
cave crickets 21
cave floor 16, 17, 18
cave paintings 24–25
cave science 28–29
caves, famous 8–9
caverns 7, 28
cavers 13, 28
caving equipment 12–13
chambers 6, 7, 9, 14, 23, 24, 27
cliffs 10
coastlines 7, 26
Coelondonta 25
columns 8, 15, 17, 18, 19
crystals 14, 15, 28

drapery deposits 19
dripped shapes 16–19
dripstone 19

echolocation 21, 28
ecosystems 29
erosion 7, 10

Fingal's Cave 8
flowstone 17, 19
fossils 29

giant elk 24
glacier caves 27
glowworms 22
headlands 7
helmets 13

Homotherium 24

ice 6, 7, 26–27
ice age 24, 25

karst 10, 11

limestone 6, 7, 10, 16, 18, 27, 28, 29

mapping caves 14–15, 29
Mammoth Cave 8
Marble Caves 9
measuring caves 14
Megaloceros 24
Mulu Caves 9

parts of a cave 6–7
passages 6–7, 9, 10, 12, 14, 15, 23, 27
photographing caves 15
prehistoric animals 24–25, 28
prey 21, 22
pseudoscorpions 21

Reed Flute Caves 9
rock 6, 7, 8, 9, 10, 12, 19, 28

saber-toothed cat 24, 25
salamanders 21
Sarawak Chamber 9
shilin 11
sinkholes 6, 10
speleologists 28, 29
speleology 28–29
speleothems 19, 27
stalactites 6, 15, 16, 17, 18, 19
stalagmites 15, 16, 17, 18, 19
straw stalactites 19
stone forest 11
streams 6, 7, 10

tides 26, 28
troglobites 20
trogloxenes 20

water 6, 7, 10, 16, 19, 21, 26, 27, 28
woolly mammoth 25
woolly rhinoceros 25